Handbook for
Adaptive Catechesis

Handbook for Adaptive Catechesis

Serving Those With Special Needs

✳ *Nurturing different abilities*
✳ *Fostering strong spirits*
✳ *Growing into the community*

MICHELE E. CHRONISTER, MA

Liguori
LIGUORI, MISSOURI

Imprimi Potest:
Harry Grile, CSsR, Provincial
Denver Province, The Redemptorists

Published by Liguori Publications
Liguori, Missouri 63057

To order, call 800-325-9521
www.liguori.org

Library of Congress Cataloging-in-Publication Data
Chronister, Michele E.
  Handbook for adaptive catechesis : serving those with special needs / Michele E. Chronister. -- 1st ed.
    p. cm.
  Includes bibliographical references (pp. 93–94).
  ISBN 978-0-7648-2145-5
  1. Church work with people with disabilities--Catholic Church. 2. Church work with students--Catholic Church. 3. Catechetics--Catholic Church. I. Title.
  BX2347.8.H34C47 2012
  268'.4087--dc23

                                                          2012016194

Liguori Publications, a nonprofit corporation, is an apostolate of The Redemptorists. To learn more about The Redemptorists, visit Redemptorists.com.

Printed in the United States of America
16 15 14 13 12 / 5 4 3 2 1
First Edition

This book is dedicated to my dear friends at Logan Center, Sharing Meadows, Little Flower Catholic Church, Misericordia (especially those in McGowan home), and St. Pius X Catholic Church. You have all taught me so much, and I will always hold you dearly in my heart.

Contents

Chapter 1

An Important Ministry

That I might not become too elated, a thorn in the flesh was given to me….Three times I begged the Lord about this, that it might leave me, but he said to me, 'My grace is sufficient for you, for power is made perfect in weakness.' I will rather boast most gladly of my weaknesses, in order that the power of Christ may dwell with me….For when I am weak, then I am strong" (2 Corinthians 12:7–9, 10b).

God's Grace, Our Weakness

This passage from Paul's Second Letter to the Corinthians appears once in the Sunday Lectionary cycle, and it just so happened to appear when I was working at a faith-based summer camp for individuals with disabilities or special needs. Having had little to no experience in this form of ministry, I was overwhelmed and humbled on a daily (maybe even hourly) basis. This passage spoke right to my experience of ministry with those with disabilities—God worked through my weaknesses to show God's strength.

As I continued in my ministry to individuals with disabilities, this passage took on new meaning. I began to see that these same words could be applied to the people I was working with, people whom the world viewed as weak and incapable. I began to think back to the stories of the saints as well as men and women from the Old Testament, and I realized that time and time again God chose to work through those the world considered weak and small.

A paramount example, of course, is the Blessed Mother. Although poor, humble, and uneducated, she was chosen by God to be the mother of Jesus, *Theotokos* (God-bearer). We can find many other examples as well. Consider Saint Bernadette, Saint Thérèse of Lisieux, or even Saint Paul. Both the Scriptures and Church history are replete with individuals the world thought little of—or even despised—and yet they were chosen by God in a very special way.

Special Needs—What to Consider

Individuals with disabilities are often forgotten and mistreated in modern society. We can fool ourselves into believing this isn't true, pointing to things like closed-captioning television and handicapped parking spaces. Beyond that, though, they are often faced with problems such as inaccessibility or lack of adequate care. Consider your church, for example. Does your sanctuary have stairs or a ramp? Even parishes that consider this ministry important and are supportive of these individuals and their families often lack this basic necessity.

This is a very simple example, but what about the more serious matters, such as the lack of adequate physical care, to say nothing of spiritual care?

I have been blessed to know many wonderful families, organizations, and residential communities that support individuals with disabilities and offer them phenomenal care. However, I have found this to be the exception rather than the rule. The families and caregivers I've worked with have shared with me that individuals with severe disabilities are often relegated to nursing homes and state-run facilities (where they have little to no stimulation and only minimal care). They've also shared with me some of the opposition those with less severe disabilities encounter in schools and parishes. Even when the physical needs of these individuals are met, often their spiritual needs are not fully understood and realized.

Many of these individuals lack the opportunity to receive adequate catechesis, such as preparation to receive the sacraments and the opportunity to attend or fully participate in Sunday Mass. This is not even considering those exceptional individuals who desire to attend daily Mass, receive the sacrament of reconciliation regularly, or have a spiritual director. Rather, this is generally the current situation for all those with disabilities and in need of very basic catechetical instruction. Wouldn't it be wonderful if we could create a vision for catechizing and welcoming these individuals on the fringes in our Church?

Called and Chosen—Members of God's Family

People with disabilities are baptized members of the Church, members of Christ's mystical body. This means that not only are they loved by Christ and are cherished members of the Church, but it also means they have a valuable role to play in the Church. Often when we are considering ministry to those with disabilities, the focus is on what we can do for them. The focus, however, should be on what they are called to do and how we can help them do it.

Rather than a ministry focused merely on inclusion, what if our ministry went a step further to focus on a more profound form of inclusion—recognizing that those with disabilities have been given a unique vocation by God? What if our ministry focused on helping them live out their baptismal call by guiding them through the process of discerning their vocation, whatever that may mean for a particular individual?

For some, it may mean helping them recognize the joy they can bring to others and how God can work through that gift. For others, it could be discerning a call to one of the few religious communities set up to accommodate vocations from individuals with disabilities, and then helping them say yes to the unique call God has given them.

This moves this form of ministry beyond the small picture with concerns about how our catechetical programs function and how to place individuals in a faith-formation classroom into a larger focus: How is this individual called by God, and what can we do to help the person do the specific work he or she is being called to do? This moves our ministry beyond the focus on logistics (which are important but cannot be the end) to the purpose of why we do what we do.

All of this makes sense in light of Saint Paul's Second Letter to the Corinthians. God chooses those the world considers small and weak to accomplish God's will. How can we support individuals with special needs on the road to sainthood? How can we acknowledge that each of these persons has a unique vocation—a role in the Church that only he or she can play? This is the context in which we will consider this ministry.

Past and Present—Understanding the Church

To understand some foundations for the respect and love we are called to show those with disabilities, we must go back to the gospels and to Christ himself. At a time when illness or disability was thought to be a punishment for personal sin, Christ acknowledged that rather than punishment, it was a form of suffering. Through his love, respect, and attention to those who were crippled, blind, deaf, and mute, Christ set a precedent for the ministry we perform today.

The Church, however, has had a long history filled with ups and downs. In previous years, those with disabilities or special needs were often not welcomed into the Church in the way they should have been. Many were denied the Eucharist, reconciliation, or confirmation because they were thought to be incapable of understanding these sacraments. Much of this was a result of misunderstandings caused by the views of society. It is helpful to consider the era of the Church in which we live and what has come before.

We haven't always known as much about specific disabilities as we do now. For example, in the past those with Down syndrome were relegated to institutions where they were hidden from the rest of society. In that time period, those with disabilities were not welcome in society and probably wouldn't even have considered venturing into a church or asking for the sacraments, with the exception perhaps of baptism. The thought of having an altar server with Down syndrome was inconceivable. This doesn't excuse the fact that those with disabilities have not previously been ministered to in the way they should, but it does help place it in context.

All of this began to change in the latter part of the twentieth century. A major contributing factor to this change was that we began to know more about those with disabilities. We began to realize that they had many capabilities and gifts and deserved to be treated with dignity and respect. At the same time various Church documents began to emerge that recognized the importance of ministry for those with special needs. In both the *General Directory for Catechesis* as well as the *National Directory for Catechesis*, the bishops emphasized the utmost importance of providing for the catechetical needs of those with disabilities.

The USCCB (then the National Conference of Catholic Bishops) also came out with a wonderful document in the 1970s, *Guidelines for Celebration of the Sacraments with People with Disabilities.* In this document, the bishops give an overview of the modifications and considerations that need to be made for individuals with disabilities who are preparing to receive the sacraments. Since the release of that document, there has been an increased interest in providing catechesis for those with special needs. Even Pope Benedict XVI, in his recent Apostolic Exhortation on the Eucharist *(Sacramentum Caritatis)*, briefly highlights the importance of making the Eucharist available to those with developmental disabilities.

There is certainly an interest in performing this ministry in the Church, but what is needed now are people willing to actually undertake the challenge. Presumably, if you are reading this right now, you are hoping to become one of those people!

What's Your Role?

The importance of this ministry cannot be overemphasized, not only for the Church but also for the individual Catholic. The most obvious beneficiary—the individual with a disability—clearly is positively impacted by the efforts of those wishing to include him or her in catechetical and ministerial opportunities. Beyond that is the next tier: friends and family of those with a disability are profoundly affected as well. I can affirm from firsthand experience that friends and family of an individual with a disability are greatly strengthened in their faith when a priest, religious, or layperson shows a desire to include and serve their loved one. Choosing to do this ministry delivers a message of hope, telling them, "You are not alone… you are always welcome in the Church!" To those who often face rejection everywhere they turn in society, this is a very powerful message.

However, the effects of choosing to do ministry with and for those with disabilities extend far beyond this inner circle. Once we begin this ministry, we soon learn that not only do we have something to give these individuals, but they truly have much to give us.

Christine's Story

The story of my friend Christine (all names have been changed for the sake of privacy) illustrates this truth.

Christine, a young woman in her early twenties with moderate cerebral palsy, lives in a Catholic-run facility for individuals with disabilities. I had met her the first summer I worked at this particular residential facility following my sophomore year of college. A friend I was working with had developed a close friendship with Christine and often spoke to me about what an incredible young woman she was. It wasn't until I returned the following summer that I came to know Christine better.

My assignment that year included responsibilities in the particular home Christine lived in, as well as in the ministry office of the facility. In my conversations with her, I discovered that Christine possessed a very real faith but had lots of questions about that faith. Hers were deep questions, ones that affected the very core of her life and experience. However, always in the midst of those questions, she came back to her strong trust in God and her love for him.

In time, I had the privilege of becoming a sort of spiritual director to her (more of a spiritual friend), and we would meet throughout the week to discuss matters of faith. We went to Mass together, and once I even received special permission to take her to Mass and adoration at the parish adjoining the facility's campus. We walked together to the small Marian shrine down the road from her home, and we prayed together.

That summer I was in the midst of discerning some very large things in my own life (discerning marriage to the man who would later become my husband), and I was daily inspired by Christine and her trust in God. Even at times when things became difficult for her, she always trusted that God would provide. I became inspired to do the same, and from her I learned so much about God's love. She radiates it to everyone she meets.

The following summer Christine was a bridesmaid in my wedding, and she continues to be a good friend. This young woman truly had a special vocation from God—the gift of loving friendship and trust—and the Church (and myself!) is so much better because she has shared that gift.

Chapter 2

Addressing the Needs of Students With Disabilities

For those desiring to take on the challenge of beginning this ministry in the parish setting, a number of considerations need to be made. What sort of program will best meet the needs of your students? What resources can your parish draw on to meet those needs? (The considerations in this chapter can be applied to ministering to those with disabilities outside the parish setting, with slight modifications for your given situation.) Ultimately, this discernment process comes down to two fundamental questions: What setting will be most conducive for special-needs learning? How can the parish accommodate that need? The following methods are three possible approaches.

MAINSTREAMING

Mainstreaming is the most common way the needs of students with disabilities are met in most parish catechetical programs. This method places a student in an age-appropriate class of students without disabilities, often providing the student with an aide to assist with the workload and any behavioral difficulties. Mainstreaming is typically the most recommended method for meeting the needs of students with disabilities for two reasons—it requires little extra training for volunteers (and fewer volunteers), and it prevents the students' further isolation from their peers.

However, this method also has several drawbacks. Some students find that the average catechetical classroom setting is not conducive to their learning style, or they may experience isolation in the sense that they feel different and alone. This is especially a problem when catechists and aides misinterpret behavioral problems as misbehavior and create an unsympathetic environment for a student with special needs. When this is the case, a student may do better in a more sympathetic setting better suited to his or her learning style.

INDIVIDUAL INSTRUCTION

This option can serve as a happy medium for parishes that find themselves with too few students or not enough resources to start a separate program for individuals with disabilities. It's also an option for parishes presented with several students who are struggling in a mainstreamed setting. Individual instruction can include the use of a specialized curriculum in working one-on-one with students with special needs, or it may simply be a matter of working through the mainstreamed curriculum at a slower pace with opportunities for hands-on learning.

The advantage of individual instruction is that it affords the opportunity to adjust the teaching style and presentation of content based on one individual. Some individuals thrive in this sort of one-on-one atmosphere. However, individual instruction can be especially difficult when dealing with several students with vastly different needs. Another disadvantage of this method is that it can easily lead to isolation from other students in your parish's catechetical program. Thus it is important to include these students in all activities, such as Mass and penance services, along with the other students in the catechetical program.

SPECIAL PROGRAMS

This method is often considered either controversial or unfeasible for most parishes. One real concern often raised by some parishes is that special programming separates students who already face much separation from others in the parish community. For other parishes, the thought of a special program for students with special needs is appealing but not feasible due to concerns about staffing a separate catechetical program in addition to the parish's main faith-formation program. Furthermore, many are anxious about what a curriculum in a specialized program would look like.

These fears can be addressed and put aside, however, if certain considerations are taken into account. In my personal experience, this method—although not as widely advocated these days as mainstreaming—is often the most effective for students with special needs.

To begin with, if done properly, isolation does not occur. In fact, forming a specialized catechetical program for students with special needs can actually solve the problem of isolation for some. In a parish I previously worked in, I developed a specialized catechetical program for students with special needs, the Children of St. Angela Merici program, named for the patron saint of those with disabilities. One of the great benefits of this program was how it served as a support for all the families involved. The families of the students and the students themselves came together and bonded over shared experiences and struggles. The bonds that were formed actually helped many of them to feel more welcome in the parish.

Resources were also given to parents to allow them to fulfill their role as primary catechists in their children's lives. The students thrived in an environment in which they could relax and be themselves, surrounded by other students who could empathize with their own experience. Many of the students benefited from the hands-on approach of the program, but they also benefited from the fact that this hands-on learning occurred with other students!

In addition to all of this, the students were incorporated into the parish community as much as possible, frequently being featured in the bulletin, attending Lenten reconciliation services with other students in the mainstreamed program, and openly welcomed at Mass. One of our students even became an altar server! The fact that the pastor and parish staff completely supported the program greatly influenced its success, thus setting the tone for the rest of the parish.

The question, however, of staffing a program like Children of St. Angela Merici and determining a curriculum for such programs still remains. For some smaller parishes, forming such a program isn't feasible. In this case, if there is a need, a group of smaller parishes may form such a program together, or students from a smaller parish may be welcomed into the program at a larger parish. Even in our program, we had many students who were nonparishioners. Curriculum will be discussed in a later chapter, but suffice it to say that this need not be a hurdle if people are willing and able to run this sort of program.

Relationships and Methodology

INVOLVE PARENTS WHEN PLACING STUDENTS

In the parish in which I worked, all three of the options I've described were offered. Some students were mainstreamed into the general catechetical program. Others were learning in a one-on-one environment, and still many others were in the specialized program. How were these students placed in one catechetical setting over another?

The first consideration that must be taken into account is the opinion of the parents of a student with special needs. This is important because the parents of this child possess a wealth of knowledge about their son or daughter and can bring much insight to the question of placement. The second reason is because, when working with the parents of a student with special needs, you are entering a partnership. It is only through this partnership that the needs of the student can be met. Gaining the trust of the parents and helping them see that you respect the hopes they have for their child are of utmost importance.

In consulting with the students' parents, you will soon discover that many parents feel strongly about mainstreaming versus special programming, and still others will be open to whatever you are able to offer. Whatever side they are leaning toward, parents will respect and appreciate whatever you are able to do to accommodate their needs. This may sometimes mean having to strike a balance between the desires of the parents and your parish's resources, but it is possible to find middle ground between the two.

Some parents may fear their child will do poorly in a mainstreamed atmosphere, but the parish doesn't have the resources to start a special program. Can the student be assigned to an aide who takes him or her out of the classroom for a good portion of the class time to go over the prepared lesson one-on-one?

Other parents may greatly desire that their son or daughter experience as "normal" a faith-formation experience as possible and so are adamantly against any sort of special programming, even though you know their child may struggle in a mainstreamed environment. Perhaps the student can split time between the mainstreamed setting and the special programming. Or perhaps the student can engage in the special-programming classes but participate in the "experiences" of the mainstreamed program, such as special Masses, penance services, and sacramental-preparation retreats.

A compromise can be reached in many different ways between what a parent desires and how you feel the parish can best accommodate the needs of a particular individual with special needs.

ASSISTING CATECHISTS

In addition to discussing options with the parents of an individual with special needs, it also helps to assess your program's resources. Begin by talking to the student's potential catechist. In a mainstreamed setting, some catechists may not feel equipped to face the unique challenges that accompany teaching a little one with special needs.

In the case of special programming, it's a good idea to discuss the possible addition of a new student with the catechist. A catechist in such a program typically is very attuned to the needs of his or her students and will be able to help you discern if the class is in a place to accept another student at that particular time.

Finally, examine the curriculum. After speaking with the parents or guardians, you should have a sense of a particular student's learning style. What is the pace of the curriculum in the mainstreamed class? Is it manageable for this particular student? Is there enough repetition, hands-on activities, opportunity for questions and discussion?

What about the curriculum of your special programming? If your parish does not have special programming, is there a way to modify the mainstreamed curriculum so that the individual will be able to work in a way conducive to his or her learning style?

The bottom line of all of this is simple: Creativity is key when working with students with special needs and their families. It is very rare that a parish has nothing to offer students with special needs. At the very least, a parish may look to direct a student to the faith-formation program of another parish that may better suit his or her needs, and even offer to contact this parish on behalf of the student and his or her family. It is important to pray in the midst of all of this, and then to remain open to the solution God sends.

One final note on the subject of placement: Never turn away a child or adult with disabilities. In the midst of a world that does not value or respect human life as it should, the last thing an individual with disabilities needs is to be rejected by the Church.

This is not to say you must have a perfect solution for each student who walks through your door. It does mean you should be willing to work together toward a solution. If the special-programming class is full, perhaps the student can be put on a waiting list. If no aides are available for a mainstreamed class, perhaps you can wait-list the student until there are, and in the meantime supply the parents with materials to home-school the child. Perhaps you have a standing agreement with another parish that is better able to accommodate a student's needs. The possibilities are endless!

Chapter 3

What Are
Special Needs?

I'll admit that my academic background is in theology and not in special education, and I'm guessing most of you are in a similar place. A variety of different resources are available, including websites and books, that can help you get to know more about specific disabilities. Since this is not my area of expertise, I won't be addressing the specifics of these disabilities in this chapter. Rather, I will try to help you understand the broad spectrum of students with whom you may be working.

In my experience, when we are talking about students with special needs, we're talking about a number of different groups of people. Some students may be deaf or blind. Others may have a significant physical or developmental disability, such as cerebral palsy. Many of the students may have learning disabilities. You may also encounter a number of students with other common "special needs," including ADD/ADHD, autism spectrum disorders, and Down syndrome.

These individuals will come to you with their own unique needs. Do not let the name of a disability label a student. Rather, a diagnosis or name of a disability can help serve as a starting point in serving the student's needs. Parents or guardians may be helpful in assessing the needs of the student and in giving you advice for meeting a student's specific needs.

That being said, here are some general guidelines to keep in mind when working with students with a variety of needs.

Addressing Special Needs in the Classroom

Again, let's assume that many of you will be working with students with special needs in a faith-formation–class setting. It is important to note, however, that what we'll discuss can also be applied to other ministry settings. In the Children of St. Angela Merici program, we were blessed to have enough students and volunteers to make it possible to take students' specific disabilities into account when determining which class to place them in.

This served two purposes. First, students with similar disabilities, while not having identical needs and learning styles, do have similarities in terms of their needs. Grouping together students with similar disabilities helped the catechist and aides better navigate the waters of meeting their students' needs. Second, and equally if not more important, were the needs of the parents. We found that grouping together students with similar disabilities often had the added benefit of meeting the needs of the parents in our program. Parents with similar experiences found support and friendship as they waited for their children to finish their class session. This further enhanced the program's atmosphere of welcome and respect.

However, even if students are placed in a class with others with similar disabilities, you will still be faced with meeting a wide variety of needs. Here it helps to follow a simple piece of advice—look to the individual student, not to his or her diagnosis. Although knowing a little about the challenges your students face can be helpful, it's important to remember that your students are not defined by their disabilities. Their disabilities are a *part* of who they are, but they are not *all* of who they are.

That being said, keeping in mind some basic information about a student's given disability can be a helpful starting point when planning your lessons. Does your student have autism and learn better with pictures and story boards, for example? Or does your student have Down syndrome and do better with hands-on lessons instead of book lessons? Does your student have ADHD and thrive in an environment in which he or she is invited to move around as needed? These sorts of considerations are certainly important for planning purposes when striving to meet your students' needs.

Seeing as God Sees

The work we are doing in catechesis is not just in teaching about God but about forming faith in God. Though it is helpful to know the disability or special need a student may have in assessing how he or she may best learn, catechesis doesn't stop there. In the work of catechesis, we must come to know the student's very core. In essence, this means learning to look at a student and see what God sees. This is no small task. In fact, it is a matter for the catechist to take to prayer each day as he or she seeks the grace to truly love each student.

To illustrate, I'll tell you about one of my all-time favorite students, a little girl I'll call Sarah. Sarah is an adolescent (although she was preadolescent when I first met her) with Down syndrome. Many people possess the mistaken notion that all people with Down syndrome are sweet, docile, peaceful, and happy all the time…as if they aren't individuals with their own personalities! Sarah most certainly had a personality. She struggled with some behavioral problems, many of which were related to medical issues beyond her control. Some people saw Sarah and only noticed her behavioral problems, much to their own detriment.

This little girl was remarkable. She was intelligent, often quick to give good answers to the catechist's questions. She was compassionate, always the first to notice if something was wrong with one of the other students, the catechist, or the aides, and then asking, "[Name], what's the matter?" She was filled with a passion for life—always on the move, always ready for the next thing, wanting to help, and wanting to laugh. She brought so much life to the classroom!

Despite all of that, she did have her hard days. She had days when she wouldn't listen, days when she was distracted, days when she didn't want to come into the classroom. Some looked at her and saw only those days. However, those blessed friends of hers looked at those days and saw them for what they were—bad days that didn't define her. Sarah was so much more than her disability. At this particular parish we were truly blessed because the pastor of the parish had known Sarah since she was small and truly loved and understood her. She was a treasure to him, even on the days when she was disruptive. What an example this is to all pastors—to love as Christ loves!

Being Christ for All Students

In an ideal situation, classes are small, the number of catechists and aides is high, and each student's needs are perfectly met. In a real-world situation, this is often not plausible; many students with special needs are lumped into a group that may not be catered to their individual needs. Whether in a mainstreamed class or a specialized class, the challenge most parish faith-formation programs face is how to meet the many different needs with such a variety of students and styles of learning.

Again, this is where it's helpful to refocus on what matters in a faith-formation setting. Your aim as catechist is not to perfectly meet the needs of each student. That is an impossible task. Rather, you are called to be Christ to each of them and to help each one feel respected, loved, and wanted in your parish and in the Church. In terms of the big picture, it is important to keep this goal in mind.

There are a few things you can do to make this task a bit more manageable. First, you should take the time to interview all parents and guardians of your students with special needs—whether in person, via e-mail or phone, or by having them fill out a detailed form. Pick their brains for as much information about their children as you can. Be sure to get any relevant medical information, as well as other information, such as the student's interests, likes and dislikes. This is especially useful if you have students who are nonverbal or who have difficulty with verbalization. Although you will have a good sense of who your students are within a matter of a few classes, it helps to have a starting point.

Once you have acquired this information, share it with

your catechists and aides. They, too, will find it helpful to have a starting point when working with these students. You may also want to ask the parents or guardians of your students if they can suggest any resources to help you learn more about your students' particular disabilities.

Beyond that, patience and flexibility are key when catechizing students with special needs—or any student for that matter! It helps if you are willing to adapt your lessons and the flow of your class to meet their needs. While you will inevitably find yourself doing what you can to cater to the needs of most of your students, it is still important to consider individual needs. One thing we found helpful in the Children of St. Angela Merici program was to set aside a portion of each class for the catechist to work with each student one-on-one. This was accomplished while the other students were doing an activity with the aides.

Working one-on-one allowed the catechist to learn how to best interact with each student, and then he or she was able to apply that to the group lesson. For example, one of our students, a boy with Down syndrome, loved to help put materials in place during the lesson (he enjoyed setting up our small altar during our unit on the Mass, for example). His catechist allowed him to help in this way, and then followed up with a high-five and a round of applause for a job well done. He loved this positive affirmation, and letting him help arrange materials during the lesson helped him stay engaged.

This can certainly apply to students with special needs who are mainstreamed into your parish's general faith-formation program. Encourage catechists to set aside a few minutes—perhaps while the other students are working on an activity or maybe after class—to meet one-on-one with any students with special needs to briefly go over some of the lesson. This will help the catechists get to know an individual better, including how he or she learns. As an added bonus, this will help the catechists form a bond with their students with special needs. Isn't that what the work of catechesis is all about? Catechesis is not just about teaching the faith, but about working through our relationship with our students to help them grow in their relationship with God.

Teaching Christ's Beloved

Finally a note on working with students labeled as "higher functioning" versus "lower functioning." All that is meant by this is the severity of a disability and whether the challenges a student faces make it more or less difficult to engage in daily activities. Most catechists, even those who feel initial nervousness, would quickly feel comfortable working with a student who is "higher functioning." You may find that the challenges some of the students face don't interfere much with their ability to participate in class as any other student would. This may be what a catechist expects when working with a student with special needs—someone who is sweet and docile and blends in easily.

The reality is, as we've mentioned before, that a student with special needs is just like any one of us —someone who is living in a broken, weary world and who is very much in need of the love of Christ. Just as with anyone else, you'll find that your students with special needs may require this love and respect expressed to them in different ways at different times. Some will just know they are loved by God, and you will be able to tell how at peace they are with this knowledge. These students are the ones a catechist has much to learn from! But many will be like yourself—full of questions, fears, doubts, and stress. Even your sunniest student will have days like this.

For the students who may face greater challenges, perhaps severe developmental or physical disabilities, it is important to be very intentional about being Christ to them and seeing Christ in them. This is especially true for a student who has severe behavioral problems that are linked to his or her special needs. Don't kid yourself…this is a work of grace! To accomplish this as a catechist, you must spend much time in prayer, asking God for the grace to love those he has entrusted to your care. In our program, our philosophy was to help our students know they were truly loved in our classroom, and then we would worry about trying to teach them everything else. A person who has not experienced the love of Christ firsthand will struggle much more to believe in it and to grow into it.

All the guidelines given in this chapter can be applied to any student, regardless of the severity of his or her disability. Students with more severe disabilities may be faced with more challenges, and it may take more patience and creativity to catechize them, but it is a worthwhile endeavor! Remember, God works through those who are little and weak and forgotten by the world to do his will.

Chapter 4

Essential Components of This Ministry

Because the students you will be working with have their own set of needs and their own unique gifts to bring to your catechetical setting, it's important to keep in mind some basic guidelines.

General Guidelines From the
National Directory for Catechesis

The *National Directory for Catechesis* shares the following guidelines for providing catechesis to persons with special needs:

- Catechesis for persons with disabilities must be adapted in content and method to their particular situations.

- Specialized catechists should help them interpret the

meaning of their lives and give witness to Christ's presence in the local community in ways they can understand and appreciate.

• "Great care should be taken to avoid further isolation of persons with disabilities through these programs which, as far as possible, should be integrated with normal catechetical activities of the parish" (quoting *Pastoral Statement of U.S. Catholic Bishops on Persons with Disabilities*, 16)

• Catechetical efforts should be promoted by diocesan staffs and parish committees that include persons with disabilities. (NCD 208–209)

These guidelines are an important starting point, as they illuminate the basic concerns that need to be kept in mind when beginning this ministry. Let's look at them one by one.

• **Catechesis for persons with disabilities must be adapted in content and method to their particular situations.**

This statement is even richer than it may appear at first glance. It takes into account the fact that those with disabilities have particular learning needs not only because of their disabilities, but also because of their situations. Fleshing this out a bit more, we need to understand what considering the "situation" of a person with a disability entails. First, it is important to know the person's special needs and how those can be met. This will lend itself to a certain form of adaptation.

For example, let's say you are working with an individual with Down syndrome who functions at a moderate level and who works best with hands-on lessons. From this alone you know you may need to adapt the content of your lessons in a way that makes them more accessible. This is not the same as simplifying the content. Rather, present the lessons in a way that they can be understood and accessed without watering them down. Have hands-on materials, try keeping the lessons shorter so they do not overwhelm, and work at a slower, gentler pace, using lots of repetition.

However, this is only the beginning. Let's consider a student's age. The lessons will look very different if you are working with a seven-year-old than if you are working with a forty-year-old. What is a student's living situation? If the student lives with his or her parents, that is very different than if he or she lives with roommates or at a facility for individuals with disabilities. This living situation will affect the student's outlook on the world. Do you know anything about your student's background and life experiences? All of these factors will affect what you teach and how you teach it.

- **Specialized catechists should help them interpret the meaning of their lives and give witness to Christ's presence in the local community in ways they can understand and appreciate.**

This guideline goes hand-in-hand with the previous one. Many individuals with special needs require ministerial care that is not all that different from the care given to individuals without special needs. They have mothers and fathers, brothers and sisters, and close friends, and therefore experience all the challenges and joys that come with those relationships. Older individuals with special needs typically have a job, and younger individuals go to school, just like anyone else. They are faced with rejection, with accomplishment, and with bad days and good days, just like all others. In the midst of this, they also need the message of the Gospel. They need someone to remind them that they are loved by God and that they are called to love the Lord in return. They need to be told that God has a special plan for them and that doing God's will begins with offering all they do each day to the Lord in love.

However, how this message is given to them may vary from your typical parish-ministry approach. It may need to be given with exceedingly more patience, gentleness, and understanding (although I'm guessing we can all benefit from that sort of care!). It also means adapting lessons to use a language and a pace that your students with special needs can understand, to the best of their ability.

It helps to consider the full picture of who the student with special needs is, beyond his or her disability. This instruction can be applied to students with special needs in a mainstreamed program as well as those in a specialized program. Regardless, catechists committed to meeting a student's specific needs through an adapted method of catechesis is essential.

The last line of this guideline is most critical to understand—individuals with disabilities are called to witness to the Gospel, just as are all other members of the Church. However, each individual is called to do this in a very particular way. The job of the catechist is to help the students become aware of this call and to discern how it is that God wants them to spread the Gospel.

• **Great care should be taken to avoid further isolation of persons with disabilities through these programs which, as far as possible, should be integrated with normal catechetical activities of the parish.**

This statement does not apply only to students who aren't mainstreamed; it applies to all "persons with disabilities." For those who aren't mainstreamed in the general faith-formation program but who are in a specialized class that can better meet their needs, then it is very important that the catechist be intentional about inclusion. Careful effort should be made to include these students in group Masses or reconciliation services with other students in the faith-formation program. They should be invited to special events that occur in the parish, and the catechist may even go so far as to team up with a mainstreamed class for some special activities and projects.

Even more care needs to be taken with students who are mainstreamed to prevent "isolation." Students in a mainstreamed program may be more susceptible to the label of "different" than students in a specialized program, since those in specialized programs are with others facing similar challenges.

Consequently, this means that other students may avoid a student with special needs. Sometimes this is done out of meanness, but much of the time it's done out of lack of understanding or because the other students don't know how to behave toward a student with special needs. Thus the catechist should lead by example and treat the individual with a disability in the same way he or she treats everyone else, showing the student with special needs the same care, respect, and patience shown to every other student in the class. The catechist should be mindful of how the other students interact with the student with special needs and should make every effort to encourage healthy interactions.

- **Catechetical efforts should be promoted by diocesan staffs and parish committees that include persons with disabilities.**

Although this guideline is self-explanatory, it is the one most often ignored. How many people with disabilities do you know who are on a parish or diocesan staff? Namely, how many people do you know with developmental disabilities on a parish staff? To help individuals with disabilities feel welcome in the Church, we must encourage them and welcome them to participate in lay ministry in whatever way they are able.

A Note on Discipline

The question of discipline in your classroom is an important one, though one that may be answered differently concerning your students with special needs. Earlier we discussed the importance of seeing a student as a person rather than judging someone based on his or her disability. We also pointed out that this is especially important when it comes to working with individuals who may have some sort of behavioral problem resulting from their disability. In the case of these students, an act that is often labeled as "misbehaving" may be related to something beyond their control and may be just as frustrating for the students as it is for the catechist. Consider Billy's story.

Billy was a little boy I worked with in a parish catechetical program for about two years. I was an aide to Billy, who was mainstreamed in the general children's faith-formation program. Billy had ADHD, which meant that keeping still was very difficult for him—actually, nearly impossible at times. When I entered the picture, the director of religious education expressed the frustration everyone involved was feeling over the situation.

Billy, who had been recently diagnosed, had difficulty sitting still during the children's Mass (attended by all students before class each Sunday) and would often run around the perimeter of the room, up by the altar, and in among the choir members. Everyone found this to be disruptive and couldn't understand why Billy wouldn't just sit still when told to do so. However, Billy, like many other children with ADHD, was just not able to do so. He wasn't purposely misbehaving, and after getting to know him, I realized he was often trying to sit still but simply couldn't. I remember him actually breaking down and crying one day because he was so frustrated by his inability to sit still.

Working with Billy was my first encounter with a child with special needs in a parish catechetical setting. The parish setting is quite different than working with someone in a setting geared toward individuals with special needs (such as a L'Arche community, residential communities for people with disabilities, or a setting in which many have a working knowledge of the challenges faced by those with special needs). In a parish setting, many people know very little about special needs and often assume that a child with a disability or special needs (such as a child with autism or ADHD) is a "bad child" who "can't behave." Because of this, the job of a parish catechist or aide of a student with special needs does not just help a particular student, but teaches everyone in the parish how to welcome those with special needs.

One thing I did when working with Billy was to change the way we talked about his behavior. Rather than saying, "He didn't behave well today," I'd say, "He seemed to have a hard day, but I could tell he was trying to do what we asked." This shift in attitude helped his parents relax because they could see that I was confident in their son's abilities and viewed him with compassion rather than criticism. It also helped the DRE to change how she talked about him. This in turn seemed to affect others. Once people saw that Billy's catechist, aides, parents, and the DRE cared about him and were sympathetic toward him, it gave them permission to behave in a similar fashion.

Showing compassion and understanding to every extent possible should be the focus of disciplining a child with special needs in a catechetical setting. This does not mean a student should be permitted to behave in whatever way he or she pleases, but it does require emphasizing positive redirection over negative criticism. As is the case with many of these students with special needs, shaming them does not lead to positive results.

In fact, shaming a student with special needs may often result in even more negative behavior because it leaves the student feeling frustrated, confused, and upset. In other cases, publicly scolding a student with special needs, as is sometimes appropriate in a mainstreamed class when a student without special needs acts out, may lead the student to withdraw and feel less comfortable in the class. Even in the rare cases in which the student with special needs is actually misbehaving and not acting out because of some sort of behavioral problem, it is still better to err on the side of giving him or her the benefit of the doubt. Here is another example of a little boy with autism whom I'll refer to as Nate.

Nate was in a class I taught and was preparing to receive first reconciliation and first Communion along with the other little boys in his class (all of whom had autism). Nate struggled in the classroom setting from the very beginning. He often disrupted the class and had a difficult time coming back to the classroom after our time in the chapel. With Nate, it was often difficult to tell the difference between misbehavior and behavioral problems related to his autism. We were very fortunate, though, because Nate naturally gravitated toward one of the aides in our class. This woman would patiently stay by his side, and when he would leave the classroom or have a difficult time returning to the classroom after our chapel time, she would be the one to slowly work her way back with him.

At one point, she confided in me that she felt badly that Nate was consistently missing the portion of the class in which the lesson was presented. In talking together, we came to the simple conclusion that it was more important to gain Nate's trust and to help him see that he was loved and would be shown patience in class, no matter what his struggle was. Through this love and patience, we hoped to help him learn about God's love for him, preaching the Gospel through our actions. Nate grew to trust us and was doing much better by the end of the academic year, thanks to this catechetical adjustment.

Disciplining a student with special needs, especially in a catechetical setting, should be done with eyes turned toward the love of Christ. While this may involve gentle correction and redirection, it also involves a genuine love and care for the student, replacing our sometimes rather innate tendency to be frustrated. As we concluded in Nate's case, if all he learned about God was what he learned through our loving actions, that would be more than enough. This was the most important lesson we could teach him—that he was loved by God, especially on his most difficult days.

One final note about discipline: Never underestimate the power of laughter. This is essential when working with any child or student, but particularly when working with a student with special needs. As a catechist, you will often be overwhelmed and frustrated. Laughter is the perfect antidote for frustration. In the moments when a student does something particularly frustrating, find a way to correct him or her with gentleness and even a little levity. This will often diffuse the situation enough that your good mood will correct the behavior.

For example, one of my students would always walk in at the start of class, pick up the basket holding the twelve Apostle figures, and dump them on the floor. Rather than yell at him—since I knew he was testing my patience and chastising him directly would be counterproductive—I would correct the behavior in a funny way that made it clear that what had just occurred was not appropriate. I would say, "Those silly Apostles. Don't they know they're supposed to stay on the table? They aren't supposed to jump out all over the floor!" After this happened a few times, the student learned that I would not overreact to the situation, and he also learned that his behavior was inappropriate. Those silly Apostles began to stay in their basket on the table!

Fostering Relationships With God and Others

For some students with special needs, developing a relationship with God and others is something that comes naturally. I can think of one sunny young lady I worked with for two years—a girl with Down syndrome—who embodied this perfectly. She was loved by everyone she met, and she possessed a joyful disposition. If you'd meet her, you would quickly and correctly conclude that she knew she was beloved by God, her family, friends, and teachers. However, this was not the case with all my students.

To begin with, some students have had a previous "bad experience" with other parishioners. It may be that they were misunderstood or judged for their disability. Part of our work as a catechist and lay minister is to find a way to forge positive relationships between the students (and their families) and the rest of the parish. The simplest way to do this is to model love and respect for our students at all times, especially when we're around other people. As exemplified in the earlier story of Billy, the kindness and compassion of the catechist and aides can go a long way in modeling loving behavior for other parishioners.

The ideal solution, however, is for your pastor to be fully on board with this ministry. In the parish where I developed the Children of St. Angela Merici program, we were blessed with a phenomenal pastor who was very loving and respectful toward all our students with special needs and their families. He modeled this for the whole parish—welcoming parishioners with special needs to serve as altar servers, returning the hug of a child with Down syndrome who would often run up to him during Mass, and showing joy whenever he saw any of our students.

A priest like this is a real blessing to our Church, and there are more of them than you may think. Many priests would be glad to show this kind of love and welcome if given the opportunity. Granted, there are instances in which a pastor does not show understanding toward individuals with special needs in his parish. In this case, we must pray for those individuals who are rejected and do all we can to direct them toward parishes and pastors that will be glad to have them.

Building Relationships for Special-Needs Students

A significant component of this ministry involves the relationship formed between the student and the catechist. As was discussed earlier, it is absolutely essential that the catechist form a loving, compassionate relationship with the students with special needs. If he or she does not do this, it will be difficult for the student to trust the catechist, and the message of the Gospel will be less plausible to him or her.

Finally, there is the question of fostering a student's personal relationship with God. Because an individual's relationship with God is a work of grace, we cannot make this relationship happen. Only God can grant the grace for one to be in relationship with him.

That being said, the Lord does work with us and through us to make this happen. This is especially the case with catechists. God calls catechists to work with him in a particular way to foster their students' relationship with him. In addition to praying for their students, catechists can create an atmosphere in their class that is conducive to a student's growing in relationship with God.

To begin with, all catechists and aides should be strongly encouraged to be gentle and calm in the classroom, as an atmosphere of calm and quiet will help the students with special needs to feel safe. This sense of security often creates a foundation of trust, which allows the students not only to trust their catechist but also to realize that they can trust God. In addition to creating this sort of atmosphere, catechists should give the students ample opportunity for prayer—both group and individual—as time allots, ideally including time with Jesus in the Eucharist.

Students who are treated with dignity and love come to know of their tremendous value as children of God. Remember, our primary goal is to help our students come to know God's tremendous love for them. We preach this not only by what we say but by how we treat them.

When trying to help foster a student's relationship with God, one thing is certain—God's work runs deeper and quieter than we can see. This is especially important to remember when working with a student who may have significant disabilities, especially the inability to verbally communicate. Although it may seem to us that nothing is being accomplished, we must trust that God is always silently working in the hearts of our students.

Parents—the Primary Catechists

Parents are the first catechists, the primary educators in the faith. A catechist should not assume the sole responsibility for catechizing a student with special needs, but should involve the parents as much as possible. This involvement will look different from case to case, depending on the situation. If periodic parent meetings (we used to have group parent meetings at the start of each new unit in the Children of St. Angela Merici program) are possible, they should certainly be held. Meetings between the parents and catechists allow everyone to be on the same page when it comes to the faith formation of the students. Parents often want to know what their children are learning and how they can help them learn better, but they need assistance in doing that.

There are a number of other ways to involve parents in the process of catechizing their children. Work sent home with the students helps parents know what is being discussed from week to week. It should be noted that it is often not practical to mandate that this homework be completed and returned. This becomes a source of stress for parent and child. It is more helpful to offer it as an additional tool. Handouts, either sent home with the child or given out at a parent meeting, can summarize the core of your lessons and serve as a "refresher course" for parents on various teachings of the faith. A parish website can post additional resources for parents of children with special needs.

Above all, it is important to remember that the work we are doing is meant to assist the parents in the work they are doing. This is an oft-forgotten point in the world of catechetical ministry. It is easy to get caught up in the work at hand, the work of imparting the faith to the students entrusted to us. Ultimately, however, it is not our responsibility to be the primary catechists for our students but that of their parents. This is not to say we shouldn't do our job, and do it well, but it does highlight the importance of giving parents—especially parents of children and adults with special needs—the resources they need. As catechists, we are called to empower and encourage parents in their role as their child's first educators in the faith. As is the case with our students, the more compassion and understanding we can show toward the parents and guardians of our students, the more we will be able to assist them in this all-too-important job.

Chapter 5

Student Needs, Parish Needs

A common question raised by directors of religious education is how to identify students with special needs. Some parents and guardians are eager to identify their child. Often the parents of a child with special needs will approach the director of the faith-formation program or the pastor of the parish, seeking catechesis and/or sacramental preparation for their child. However, this is not always the case. If you are not approached directly by a parent or guardian of someone with special needs, how else can you identify those in need of catechesis?

As previously stated, there are two different areas to consider: (1) students in a mainstreamed program and (2) students in a specialized program. Although there are some overlapping considerations, there are unique guidelines to keep in mind for each of these groups.

Students with special needs who are mainstreamed may

already be in your parish's faith-formation program. However, it may be that their needs are not being acknowledged and met. One very simple way to identify who these students are is to include a question about special needs on your faith-formation program's registration form. If you identify any students with special needs from your registration forms, it is then helpful to contact parents and guardians directly to ask more specific questions as to how best meet their child's or adult's needs.

Some parents and guardians may not identify their child as having special needs because their child may have gone undiagnosed or because they are trying to bypass the stigma surrounding individuals with disabilities. In this case, it may be helpful to regularly check in with your catechists and ask them if they have concerns about any specific students. If a particular student seems to be struggling, don't be afraid to investigate further. Remember, your role is not just to teach these students but also to support them and their families in whatever way you can.

This may be a difficult subject to approach with parents, and it should be done very delicately. One way is to contact the parents or guardians directly and ask if they have some time to meet with you after dropping off their child for the religious-education session. Make sure to approach the subject from a positive perspective, highlighting the child's strengths. Rather than saying, "We've been having problems with your child," simply say, "We're concerned that we may not be meeting your child's needs because…"

Open the door for a dialogue with the parents and take the approach of desiring to meet the needs and expectations of both parents and child. This first conversation is about instilling trust and a sense of partnership, assuring the parents that you desire what is best for the child and that you want to work with them to achieve precisely that.

This sort of conversation is important to have even in the case of parents who have self-identified their children. When working with students with special needs, the challenge of meeting their unique needs should be the topic of an ongoing conversation with their parents and caregivers.

Specialized Programs

In terms of identifying students who may do well in a specialized program, a number of different approaches can be taken. First, the program should be presented in a positive light. Rather than being offered as something remedial or for students who can't do the work in the parish's mainstreamed program, market the specialized program as yet another option for meeting the needs of all the students. Emphasize that the specialized program uses a different pedagogical approach (more hands-on) and a small catechist-student ratio. Presenting the program as a unique opportunity for students will make it more appealing to prospective students and their families.

However, this is not something that can simply be advertised in the bulletin; it requires personal invitation and conversations to recruit students to this sort of program. It is good to note, though, that a bulletin announcement can be used and will sometimes yield some wonderful responses. A good place to start is tapping in to local resources for people with disabilities. Does your diocese have an Office of Disabilities? Are there local support groups for parents and families of those with disabilities? Is there a local day program for adults with disabilities? Organizations like these can help get the word out about the catechetical and pastoral opportunities offered in your parish.

Maintaining, Envisioning, and Creating

The big step is recruiting those first few students. Typically, once you have recruited a few students into your catechetical program, whether mainstreamed or specialized, your most essential task will be to help them stay in the program. If you meet their needs, and meet their needs well, then these students and their families will spread the word about your program.

In the parish where we started the Children of St. Angela Merici program, the number of classes we offered grew exponentially in the span of about two years. Previously only one class was offered, but by the end of two years, five classes were offered to accommodate the needs of all our students. Being open to welcoming students who are not parishioners will also help your program grow. Developing a partnership with other smaller parishes and letting them know about the programs you are offering allows them to refer students to your parish's ministry.

Some of you may find yourselves with the opposite problem. Parents and guardians of individuals with disabilities may approach you and you may not have a program established for students with special needs, or you may not have aides available for mainstreamed students. In moments like these, it's best to say a prayer to the Holy Spirit and start discerning in what direction your parish is being called. It may be that you are called to establish a relationship with another parish offering resources for individuals with special needs rather than starting your own program. It may be that you are being called to meet the needs of these students in your parish, and this is where this book can be of help.

Identifying Catechists and Aides

The next challenge is identifying catechists and aides who have the necessary gifts to work with students with special needs. Again, the first step is taking this to prayer. Again and again we were called to do this in the Children of St. Angela Merici program, and God always had a way of providing—or as a colleague of mine would say, "sending workers for the vineyard."

The second step is a mixture of general announcements, such as a write-up in the bulletin or on the parish website and personal invitation. Not every person is called to this particular ministry. Let's consider the ideal characteristics of a catechist or aide for those with special needs.

Patience. A catechist or aide of individuals with special needs must be a patient person, willing to wait as students complete tasks at their own pace.

Understanding. A catechist or aide of these students must have a capacity for understanding. This, combined with patience, is absolutely essential when it comes to disciplining in a catechetical environment. A catechist or aide who is understanding will be concerned with showing students the love of Christ—an essential attribute for catechesis.

Flexibility. A catechist or aide who is flexible will be open to using whatever pedagogies will work best with the students, even if they do not fit the classic classroom mold. A catechist or aide who is flexible will also be willing to bend the rules when it comes to students with special needs—that is, willing to give them more breaks, let them have the opportunity to do more hands-on type work than other students, and so forth.

A real love for students with special needs. In doing catechesis with students with special needs, part of the catechesis requires a traditional pedagogy—lesson plans, activities, and homework. However, especially for those students who may struggle to grasp the doctrine being taught, the most important lesson that can be taught is love. Through the loving and compassionate actions of the catechist, these students can learn about the love of God and learn how to emulate that love to the best of their ability.

A real relationship with God. We cannot give what we don't have. It is absolutely essential that a catechist or aide of students with special needs have a strong prayer life. You can encourage this and even offer them resources and opportunities for deepening their prayer life.

Although all of these characteristics are well and good, it is often very difficult to identify them in a person from the outset. Trust in the work of the Holy Spirit and follow your instincts. You may intuitively sense that certain individuals are not suited to the ministry of being a catechist or an aide of a student with special needs. However, there are still many ways to get an interested individual involved, such as helping with the critical behind-the-scenes work that is necessary when preparing lessons and materials. However, some individuals may appear not to have the right characteristics at the outset and end up being fantastic catechists and aides. Be open to the gifts each individual may have, and when possible, meet one-on-one with potential catechists and aides to get a better sense of the gifts they have to bring to your program.

Training Catechists and Aides

The training of catechists and aides will differ based on your program. For example, training catechists and aides for a specialized program may be a more lengthy process than training for a mainstreamed program. However, some things are necessary regardless.

Unless you know otherwise, assume that the individual you've recruited may not know a lot about working with people with disabilities. One of the first questions to ask on an information form for potential volunteers is whether they have any previous experience working with individuals with special needs. If they do, find out more about their background experience, and do what you can to build on the knowledge they already possess.

It will also be helpful if you prepare a packet ahead of time that includes various articles, parish or diocesan guidelines, and online and book resources that can answer any questions they may have. You may even wish to provide them with *this* book! Be careful to select resources that give basic, straightforward information rather than opinions and theories that will only confuse potential catechists. A list of such helpful articles and books can be found at the end of this book.

It's also helpful to conduct training sessions in person. If you are only training one person to be an aide in your mainstreamed program, then you may be able to meet with him or her one-on-one to go over information in the training packet. However, if you need to train a larger number of catechists or aides, whether for ministry in a mainstreamed or specialized program, it will probably be more practical to hold an actual training session.

Either way, follow-up is key. Catechists and aides working in this ministry must know that they have support from others on the parish staff and that they have someone to turn to with questions. If the director of religious education does not feel equipped to field some of those questions, he or she may wish to find another individual, perhaps someone in the diocesan office, who may have more expertise in the area. A strong support network is key to being successful in this ministry!

Finally, you may wish to consider having new catechists and aides observe someone already engaged in the ministry. In the Children of St. Angela Merici program, we had new catechists observe several lessons taught by more seasoned catechists. After that, each new catechist would then present lessons with a more seasoned catechist observing, allowing the new catechists to teach on their own as soon as they felt comfortable doing so. Even after they were teaching lessons on their own, the seasoned catechists remained available as a resource. This gradual easing in helped the new catechists feel more comfortable and confident.

Selecting a Method

The question of whether to mainstream students with special needs or create a specialized catechetical program for them is best left to the discretion of the parish. Each parish will have different needs and resources.

Smaller parishes often do not have the resources to accomplish special programs. However, with a supportive pastor and willing volunteers, even a smaller parish can develop or utilize an already developed specialized program. It may be that the parish, whether larger or smaller, only has higher-functioning students with special needs who all desire to be mainstreamed into the general religious-education program. Or it may be that the students and families of those with special needs desire a smaller, one-on-one catechetical experience.

Either way, your parish or diocese should aim to practice two basic principles. First, never turn away a student. Perhaps you do not currently have the resources to accommodate a particular student with special needs. It is perfectly all right to be honest about that with his or her parents. In this situation, it is best to take down the student's contact information and tell the parents or guardians you'll be in touch. Then take the initiative to see if there is some way to accommodate the student either at your parish or at another local parish. You may even want to anticipate this possibility by contacting the diocese and some other parishes ahead of time to get a sense of what is available in your area for students with special needs. That way, even if you cannot meet their needs, you will be able to offer available options.

Second, don't get so concerned with trying to offer the perfect program that you don't offer any program until yours is just right. It is far better to offer something for students with special needs in the parish—even if what is offered is still in the process of development—than to neglect their spiritual needs. I have met numerous parents who have gone to more than one parish looking for a catechetical program that will accept their child. When these families find someone willing to welcome their child into the parish's catechetical program, it gives them so much hope—hope that their child truly does have a place in the Church. Always be willing to offer families that hope.

Integrating Into Parish Life

One of the primary goals for all students enrolled in a parish's catechetical program is to become fully integrated into the Church's life. This is true on a number of levels, and is no less true for students with special needs. These students are called to be integrated into parish life to the best of their ability. Consider what each person has to offer—from being an altar server and lector to being a greeter or to the simple but ever important task of being a full and active participant at Mass. All are called to be integrated into the diocese, whether through diocesan initiatives for people with disabilities or through participation in diocesan events and groups. They are called to be full and active participants in the Church because they bring gifts no one else can bring and because they are children of God. These students, as unique members of the body of Christ, have their own unique role to play. It is the work of catechists and pastors to discern how best to enable those with special needs to play out their role in the Church and be open to the manifestation of their giftedness in the life of the Church.

Chapter 6

Lesson Planning

To build a strong framework for your catechetical lessons, careful planning is a must. However, lesson planning for students with special needs differs essentially in that it is not just about what is taught, or even how it's taught, but about keeping in sight the goal of coming to know God through the lessons. That being said, it is important to present the doctrine of the faith in all its fullness to students with special needs. However, the doctrine must not be presented without an eye to whom the doctrine helps us to better know—God!

All must be presented with the goal of coming to know, love, and serve God. In that light, presenting doctrine to students makes more sense. The doctrine of the faith is not being presented to them because they must know it to get to heaven. Rather, we present them the fullness of the beautiful teachings of the Church in hopes that these teachings will help them get to heaven where they may be one with God, fully relying on God's grace to accomplish this. Indeed, this is what catechesis is meant to look like for all students, but especially for students with special needs.

To accomplish these lofty aims, we must consider both the content and the pedagogy.

Content

When working with students with special needs, there is a tendency sometimes to water down content so that they can understand it, but this often deprives these students of coming to know the fullness of the Catholic faith. When planning lessons or selecting a prepared curriculum for students with special needs, the question we need to ask is not, "What can they understand?" but rather, "How can I help them understand this?"

The goal is always accessibility, not simplifying. Rather than omitting certain doctrines because they seem to be too difficult for the students to understand, it is important to find creative ways to help students understand what is being presented. This may mean using hands-on materials or carefully worded definitions, art activities, song, or the like. Creativity is key in helping to make the content accessible. Of course, sometimes that creativity can take as simple a form as sitting with your student and explaining something slowly and carefully and welcoming questions. The way this looks will vary based on the needs of individual students.

On occasion you may work with a student whose mental disabilities are so severe that he or she cannot grasp what you are presenting. Even in this case, it is best not to oversimplify. Yes, you should repeat the most basic teachings of the faith over and over again to these students, reminding them particularly of the love of God, but what you teach them must not stop there. Even students with more severe disabilities have a right to be offered the faith in all its fullness, and we must trust the Holy Spirit to guide their hearts as they listen to what is presented.

The emphasis when presenting this content should be on the beauty of our faith while simultaneously remaining true to what it teaches. For example, let's consider what should be included when presenting the doctrine of the Eucharist.

The teaching of the Eucharist is twofold. First, there is an emphasis on the meal part of the Eucharist—the fact that the Eucharist was established at the Last Supper and through it we are fed by the Body and Blood of Christ. However, there also needs to be an emphasis on sacrifice, the fact that the sacrifice of Christ on the cross is re-presented (made present again) each time the Mass is celebrated. Both parts of this doctrine are necessary to present the fullness of this teaching. It is also important to emphasize that a unique union with God is experienced in the reception of the Eucharist.

Precision of language is also necessary when presenting the fullness of the faith. We can refer to the host as bread prior to the consecration, but we shouldn't use the word *bread* once it has been consecrated, for we believe it becomes the Body of Christ. A cradle Catholic may let slip *bread* when he or she actually means Body of Christ. By bread, he or she may be referring to the Bread of Life, a title of the Eucharist, or may just be using the wrong language to speak about the Eucharist. Nevertheless, a cradle Catholic will typically confirm that the Eucharist is really Jesus, even if he or she cannot explain how.

When working with students with special needs as well as

students in general, we must be very careful and precise when talking about doctrine. This is not a matter of being strict in adhering to the rules so much as lovingly being committed to preventing confusion about the teachings of the Catholic faith. For someone hearing about the Eucharist for the first time, or even preparing to receive the sacrament for the first time, incorrect terminology can cause a good deal of confusion.

For example, when explaining how the consecration occurs, we want to help students learn that before the consecration occurs, the host is just bread. However, when the priest says the words of consecration, the bread becomes the Body of Christ. The accidents remain (that is, it still looks and tastes like bread), but the substance has completely changed. It is no longer bread but is really and truly Christ, fully present in his Body, Blood, Soul, and Divinity.

Keeping all of this in mind, when you present the doctrine of the Eucharist to students with special needs, you want to present the fact that the Eucharist is both a meal and a sacrifice and that in the Eucharist, the bread and wine truly become the Body and Blood of Christ. Some would present this teaching by saying something like, "In the Eucharist the bread becomes Jesus. So when you receive the Eucharist, Jesus is inside of you." There is some truth to that statement; the bread does become Jesus, and Jesus does come inside of us in the Eucharist. However, do you see how much is missing when the doctrine of the Eucharist is presented in this way?

Contrast it with the following accessible yet rich presentation: "In the Eucharist, the bread and wine become the Body and Blood of Jesus. They may still look and taste like bread and wine, but we know they are really Jesus because Jesus told us so—and we can trust Jesus! Jesus gave us the gift of the Eucharist at the Last Supper, and we call the Eucharist a meal because this is where Jesus feeds us with his Body and Blood. However, the Eucharist is also a sacrifice because the real love of Jesus on the cross is made present to us again in the Eucharist. It is as if we are standing at the foot of the cross and Jesus is loving us just like he did then!" Stating the teaching in this way breaks it down and keeps it simple but also ensures that the fullness of the teaching is conveyed. Of course, this statement can be presented with hands-on materials to aid in understanding—a picture of the Last Supper or a crucifix to talk about meal and sacrifice, for example.

Pedagogy

The pedagogy—or *how* material is presented—is just as important as the content. To understand how we are called to catechize those with special needs, it helps to reflect a bit on divine pedagogy. The *National Directory for Catechesis* beautifully explains divine pedagogy,

"God's own methodology engages persons and communities in light of their circumstances and their capacity to accept and interpret Revelation. God's self-communication is realized gradually through [God's] actions and...words. It is most fully achieved in the Word made flesh, Jesus Christ.... This is the pedagogy of God. It is the source and model of the pedagogy of the faith" (28).

To emulate divine pedagogy when working with students with special needs, the approach must be a gradual one. Slowly building on the basics of the faith, the curriculum should include plenty of repetition and the flexibility needed to adjust to the students' pace. It should also be gradual in the sense that the students should not be rushed through the content—they must feel a sense of gentle calm as they move through each lesson. This is best achieved by aiming not to present too much during a given lesson, but to plan on presenting a small amount of material each week. It must also be gradual in the sense that the catechist and aides must be attuned to the slow and steady work God is accomplishing in each student.

Catechesis is about so much more than an intellectual learning process; it is about a real, ongoing conversion of heart. Catechists and aides must be aware of this and be willing to alter their lesson plans when it becomes clear that God is leading the class in a particular direction. For example, let's say that one day you begin class time with a few minutes spent in the church, fully intending to return to the classroom for a lesson. However, it quickly becomes clear that your students are drawn to being with Jesus in the Eucharist that day, that they have questions or are enjoying being with him for a while and praying together. The invitation here is to be open to the gradual work God is doing in these students, and thus to set aside the planned lesson until later.

The *National Directory for Catechesis* also reminds us that God engages people in light of their circumstances. This is especially relevant to settings with students who have special needs. As these students have varied and often complicated circumstances, imitation of divine pedagogy necessitates that we do what we can to take those circumstances into account. This colors the entire catechetical lesson—everything from what is discussed to how you address your students, what questions they have, how you answer those questions, what you pray for together, and so forth.

The true beauty of the Incarnation is that God comes to

meet us where we are but doesn't want us to stay there! God calls us to be in union with the blessed Trinity, God's self. Our pedagogical approach should reflect that. Although we begin by meeting our students where they are—with a simplified approach and knowledge of and sensitivity to their unique situations and needs—we must not stop there. Those catechizing students with special needs are called to draw these students ever more deeply into the mystery of our Catholic faith.

This begins with entering into the life of the sacraments and Scripture. Because of this, it is of utmost importance that students with special needs be invited to partake in the life of the sacraments to the best of their ability, and also that they be fully exposed to Church Tradition and the beautiful words of Scripture. This is why the teachings of the faith must not be watered down. The Scriptures should be presented as they are rather than paraphrased, and each lesson should include a reading from the Word of God.

Presenting the materials in an engaging way enables the catechists and aides not only to meet those with special needs where they are but also to draw the students on to something deeper. The ultimate goal of a catechist is to help his or her students understand that while the world is a beautiful place, it remains imperfect and in need of God. The world is not our true home, it is only our journeying place. We are made for God and for life with God in heaven.

If one bears this in mind, then the struggles, sufferings, and frustrations of this world, along with all the beauty and joy, can be seen in the right light. All of these realities are a part of our journey ever closer to God, who calls us to grow in love, emulating Christ. What a beautiful and hopeful message this brings to those who often experience frustration, rejection, and even suffering, reminding them that they are God's beloved children and are made for divine union with the holy Trinity! By God's grace working through each of us, we make this journey together.

Lesson Planning for Mainstreamed Students

It is not practical to expect a catechist of a mainstreamed class to prepare two separate lesson plans—one for his or her students without special needs and one for those with special needs. However, the catechist in a mainstreamed classroom should do his or her best to remain aware of the students with special needs. This means having a sense of whether they are able to keep up with the pace of the lesson and whether they need supplemental activities or need to be engaged in the lesson in different ways. Regular communication between the aide of a student with special needs and the catechist is important. The catechist may need to prepare a special activity that is better catered to how the student with special needs learns (more hands-on, for example) or may need to make an effort to periodically ask this student questions throughout the lesson.

The focus should be on helping the student to take part in the lesson in whatever way he or she is able yet also trying to challenge the student. For example, giving a sixth grader with special needs a coloring sheet to work on during the lesson—even if it's loosely connected with the theme of the lesson—is not sufficient. However, giving the student some pictures that relate to the lesson to help him or her stay focused on what is being discussed, then offering a hands-on activity, perhaps in this case a coloring sheet that is age-appropriate and includes an abbreviated explanation of the lesson or some simple questions about the lesson could be helpful. The goal here relates to imitation of divine pedagogy—the goal is not only to meet the student where he or she is at but also to draw him or her beyond and ever deeper into our beautiful faith.

Lesson Planning for Students in Specialized Programs

When planning lessons intended solely for students with special needs, more options are available. The entire class can be structured around the needs of these students in a way that is impossible in a mainstreamed class. The lesson can move at their pace and engage them in ways that are conducive to their learning styles.

The lesson plan for a specialized catechetical program should follow the same basic structure from week to week. For example, in the Children of St. Angela Merici program, we observed the following schedule:

Opening Prayer
(Included our class song and a simple prayer)

Gospel/Scripture Time
(The class would visit Jesus in the tabernacle and listen to a brief passage from Scripture)

Lesson or Story
(Lesson or "story" for the day was presented)

Activity
(Students worked on a hands-on activity, typically an art-related activity or simple worksheet, with the aides while the catechist met one-on-one with each student to review the lesson)

Closing Prayer
(A brief prayer and the class song again)

A large laminated storyboard with a printed copy of our schedule was displayed at the front of the class, and the storyboard would be referred to throughout the lesson. Although the contents of our lesson changed from week to week—different topics were presented, different activities created, and different Scripture listened to—the basic schedule stayed the same.

Two very important components should be included in these lessons if at all possible. First, students should have the opportunity to spend time with Jesus in the Eucharist by visiting him in the tabernacle, even if only briefly. This time helps them develop their relationship with Jesus and grow in Christ's love for them. Second, a passage from Scripture, even a very short passage, should be read together. This helps form the habit of Scripture reading in the students and allows them to listen to the beautiful, inspired words of God. These two practices allow your students to be open and ready for God to speak to their hearts.

Visual Aids and Other Materials

The materials, or teaching and visual aids, used in each lesson by students with special needs vary greatly from parish to parish and from class to class. The first issue is financial resources or those materials a parish can afford to purchase or make. Larger parishes may be able to afford more elaborate hands-on teaching aids, whereas smaller parishes may have to settle for something smaller and simpler. Needless to say, the generosity of parishioners can certainly go a long way, even when the budget of a parish catechetical program cannot.

The second consideration are the learning needs of the students. When the term *hands-on materials* is used, many people automatically think this means using art supplies and similar activities. For many students with special needs, these sorts of activities work really well. Activities like painting, sculpting with nontoxic clay, and coloring that are aimed at helping the class reflect on what was presented during the lesson can certainly help some students better grasp what is being taught. However, for some students these sorts of materials are more a source of frustration than a useful pedagogical tool. Know your students and their needs, and don't be afraid to try different activities together.

For materials inspiration, I strongly encourage you to do some reading about the Catechesis of the Good Shepherd (http://www.cgsusa.org) pedagogy. This beautiful program is Montessori inspired and uses hands-on materials to teach children about the faith. Its materials are exactly the kind of catechetical materials that work well for students with special needs.

The Children of St. Angela Merici program was inspired by the Catechesis of the Good Shepherd program and their wonderful hands-on materials. To give you a sense of what I mean by hands-on materials, let's examine the materials used for the Advent unit of the Children of St. Angela Merici program.

The focus of this particular unit was on Advent as a season of waiting for the coming of Christ—both in waiting for the celebration of the Incarnation that took place more than two thousand years ago and in preparation for when Christ comes again. Throughout the season, we used an Advent wreath and candles to mark the current week. Each lesson began with lighting that week's candle and a prayer.

To focus on the coming of Christ in the Incarnation, we used a Jesse Tree (the "family tree" of Jesus) to help students see the lineage of Christ through Scripture and images, and we also prayed the O Antiphons.

Here is what a typical Children of St. Angela Merici lesson for Advent looks like.

THE ENVIRONMENT

The students enter the room to find it set up with a circle of chairs and a prayer table at the front [a standard setup]. The prayer table is covered in purple, a reminder of the liturgical color used during the season of Advent. An Advent wreath with three purple candles and one rose [pink] candle sits on the table. The candles are not yet lit but soon will be.

Beside the Advent wreath is a small green Christmas tree, and in front of this small tree is a wooden box painted purple and gold (purple for Advent and gold to remind us of the King for whom we are preparing—the birth of Jesus). Inside the wooden box are small wooden coins, painted with images of different biblical figures or symbols of these figures from the Jesse Tree. A hole is drilled in the top of each wooden coin and a purple ribbon laced through so that the images can be hung on the Jesse Tree.

Tucked inside the box also are small laminated purple prayer cards. On one side of each prayer card is the name of a biblical figure from the Jesse Tree, along with a picture that represents him or her. (For example, a picture of an expectant mother for the Blessed Mother and a picture of a slingshot for David.) On the reverse side is a short verse from Scripture about this figure. The students know they will be asked to help hang the wooden coins on the tree and may take turns holding the prayer cards. At the base of the table is a basket with a Bible and a priest doll, dressed in purple vestments.

Finally, there is the O Antiphon board found at the base of the prayer table. This long, thin board is painted white with the title *O Antiphons* painted across the top. Below the title, eight small wooden squares are attached to the board with Velcro. On the first is painted the words, "O come..." and following is a square for each O Antiphon, with the title for Christ painted on it and a representative picture beneath it. (For example, for the title "O Dayspring," a small sunrise is painted on the wooden piece.) The students pray a simple version of the O Antiphons together while helping to attach each wooden piece to the board and praying, "O come, O come, O Dayspring..." (which can be sung to the traditional hymn "O Come, O Come, Emmanuel").

THE LESSON BEGINS

The students all seat themselves in the circle, and then the lights are dimmed and the candles lit. The lesson is about to begin.

Can you imagine what a beautiful and rich environment this is for students with special needs? The room is very plain other than these lesson materials, so their attention is drawn to the materials gathered by the catechist.

All of their senses are engaged—the sight of the beautiful materials, the sound of the prayers and Scriptures, the touch of the materials as they help put them in their proper place during the lesson, and the smell of the burning candles. The only thing missing is the sense of taste, and even that could be worked in with some imagination on the part of the catechist. For example, when talking about the feast of Saint Nicholas during the Advent season, the catechist could give each child a candy cane and talk about his bishop's staff. The themes being presented are challenging to understand, as not all Catholic adults even know about the O Antiphons or the Jesse Tree. However, this important teaching can be made accessible to the students by utilizing interactive materials. The classroom is a warm, welcoming environment where the students are invited and expected to help in the presentation of the lesson.

This is the type of atmosphere you are hoping to achieve in a catechetical space for students with special needs: one that is accessible, challenging but engaging, creative, beautiful, and welcoming.

Curriculum

Finally, there is the consideration of curriculum. Some pre-prepared programs are available for students with special needs, but not very many. Keep in mind, however, that a pre-prepared program may or may not suit the needs of your parish or students anyway. If possible, purchase or borrow some curricula or consult with your local diocese to get a sense of what needs to be included in your lessons.

A common but false assumption is that students with special needs don't need to be taught everything as students who do not have a disability. This assumption often results in simplified lesson plans with a lack of rich material. However, the goal of a catechist or coordinator of a program for students with special needs is to present the faith in all its richness and to do so in a way that is accessible to the students.

A wonderful example of this besides the Children of St. Angela Merici program is the Rose Fitzgerald Kennedy program (http://nafim.org/tip-sheets/). This catechetical program intended for students with special needs does an excellent job of extensively covering the teachings of the faith. The curricula is available on loan from many diocesan offices. Even if you do not strictly adhere to the lessons presented in a pre-prepared program such as these two, they will help you determine what should be presented in your classroom. Contact the diocesan office as a resource and request their curriculum guidelines.

Remember also not to worry about presenting your lessons perfectly; just take the plunge and start preparing the lessons. It's better to have lessons in a state of development than to have students with special needs lacking catechesis in your parish.

Chapter 7

Sacramental Preparation

One of the most debated and often-sought aspects of ministry for those with disabilities is sacramental preparation. Questions abound as to who is capable of receiving various sacraments and how to prepare these individuals. Before working through the logistics of sacramental preparation, however, let's consider how vocation plays in to this discussion. As is the case with all those preparing to receive the sacraments, our focus must be shifted away from looking at the sacraments as merely rites of passage to understanding them as necessary aids in living out one's baptismal call.

Addressing Vocation

When we hear the word *vocation*, any one of a number of images may come to mind. Some may imagine vocation as the priesthood, religious life, married life, or single life. Others may think of vocation in terms of the line of work an individual is called to perform. Either way, individuals with special needs and developmental disabilities are often left out when considering vocation.

The work of discerning a vocation is as real for those with disabilities as it is for anyone else. Vocation is the Lord calling an individual to respond to God in love. Our vocation is ultimately where we will find the most joy and truly be ourselves. Many people worry about picking the wrong vocation and deliberate indefinitely, afraid to commit. However, a better approach to discernment is to trust in God's loving goodness, knowing that the Lord will give you the grace to see what you were created to be and do. A vocation is a gift—a beautiful gift from God—enabling us to truly love others and fully experience and actively participate in God's love.

Presenting vocation in this context is vital to an individual with special needs or a developmental disability. Rather than skirt around the topic of vocation, thinking, *This person could never be a priest, so I won't mention vocation,* or *I know this person could never get married, so I'll just avoid talking about vocation,* it is important to recognize that each individual does have a vocation. Although many individuals with special needs are called to the single life, their vocations are about so much more than a particular life commitment. Each one of them is called by God to work in the world in a unique way. Every individual is given gifts that only he or she possesses, precious gifts from God intended to help them bring God's love to the world and to embrace the love of God in their own lives.

To help individuals with disabilities truly live as full members of the Church, those who minister in the Church must do all they can to make the sacraments accessible and available. The reception of the sacraments is necessary to fully live out and embrace one's call. As catechists, we must honor the gifts God has given every person, particularly those with disabilities, and do everything possible to help them live out God's call for their lives.

Consulting Church Documents

The most useful document for understanding the requirements and guidelines necessary for sacramental preparation with those with disabilities is *Guidelines for the Celebration of the Sacraments with Persons with Disabilities*. This document can be read in full on the National Catholic Partnership on Disability website (http://www.ncpd.org). Released in 1978 by the National Conference of Catholic Bishops, the document begins with an overview of general guidelines for sacramental preparation for those with disabilities and then proceeds to discuss the specifics of each particular sacrament.

This document is a wonderful reference point for catechists preparing an individual for specific sacraments. It is especially helpful in revealing how and when it is appropriate to prepare individuals with disabilities for the reception of the sacraments. The document makes clear that the question is not whether we should prepare people with disabilities to receive the sacraments or whether those with disabilities can be allowed to receive the sacraments. Rather, it is how to prepare those with disabilities to receive the sacraments and at what stage of their lives is it appropriate to do so.

The most significant point from the document is that the sacraments should be made readily available to those with disabilities. Although specific considerations may need to be kept in mind in the preparation process, if the question arises as to whether someone should be permitted to receive the sacraments, the favor of reception should predominate. The document makes clear that all are called to baptism, especially those with disabilities. By right of their baptism, individuals with disabilities are called to partake in the sacramental life. Pastors and catechists are to do everything possible to make this life a reality.

Approaches and Considerations for Sacramental Preparation

Once individuals with disabilities began to be openly welcomed to receive the sacraments, some well-meaning individuals decided to permit those with disabilities to receive the sacraments without any real preparation. Although that is a much better option than barring these individuals from receiving the sacraments, something was still missing. The missing link was the opportunity to learn about the mystery they received through the sacraments, though this problem is not without remedy, as I have seen some beautiful and successful mystagogy done with students with disabilities who received the sacraments years ago without any preparation.

Yet there is a real opportunity for formation when this preparation is done properly. Sacramental preparation—although a serious task to undertake—is also intended to be a joyful time of waiting to encounter God in a special way. Preparation for the sacraments should always be viewed with this in mind.

How and when a student with special needs is prepared to receive various sacraments depends on the student's particular needs. Some students with special needs will be able to receive various sacraments at the same time as their mainstreamed counterparts. Other students will need a much longer period of preparation. Whenever possible, students with special needs should not be made to wait longer than their friends without special needs to receive the Eucharist, the sacrament of reconciliation, or confirmation.

Some sacraments require little to no preparation. For example, all should receive the sacrament of baptism, and as an infant if possible. In this case, more energy is typically focused on the parents and godparents, and what they learn will prepare them to raise their child or godchild in the faith. The sacrament of anointing of the sick needs no extraneous preparation. Depending on the severity of their disability, and also dependent on their vocation, some people with disabilities may never receive the sacraments of matrimony or holy orders.

Typically in the Roman Rite, a child undergoes preparation to receive reconciliation and the Eucharist at some point around the age of reason. In the United States, it is also common for people to receive confirmation at some point in adolescence, usually late middle school or early high school. The catechist and parents, working under the guidance of the pastor, can best determine whether a child with special needs is ready to receive these sacraments at the same time as his or her peers. Indicators of readiness will vary based on the child, but note that not all individuals with disabilities are able to verbally communicate their beliefs. Especially in these cases, the catechists must take particular care to determine how best to undertake sacramental preparation.

Sacraments of Initiation—Some Key Focal Points

Bearing in mind the tips given for lesson planning, let's explore the essential doctrines that should be taught when preparing a student with disabilities to receive the sacraments for the first time.

BAPTISM

Baptism is the very first sacrament. Preparation for baptism will often just involve a review of the teachings of the Church on this sacrament and the responsibilities of parents and godparents. Those catechizing parents of a baby or child with special needs should emphasize to the parents that their little one is welcomed and cherished in the Church. Another important point to emphasize is that their child has a unique vocation, a particular role to play in God's divine plan. Parents and godparents can pray for the child regularly, but they should also make a point of reminding their child—from the earliest age—that he or she is called by God and loved by God.

By right of his or her baptism, an individual with disabilities should be prepared and permitted to receive further sacraments as he or she is able. Keep in mind also that if an individual with special needs is entering the Church on his or her volition, preparation for the sacrament of baptism should follow the Rite of Christian Initiation of Adults. (See page 87.)

Reconciliation is often the next sacrament for which individuals prepare and celebrate. Because a person is only obliged to receive this sacrament if he or she is in a state of serious (mortal) sin, this sacrament is not always required of an individual with special needs. Although there are some exceptions to the rule, many individuals with disabilities (particularly mental disabilities) do not have the capacity to commit a mortal sin, as one needs to have a developed reason to commit such a sin (more developed than many of those with mental and developmental disabilities possess).

That being said, the sacrament of reconciliation should nonetheless be offered to the individual. Then it can be left to the discretion of the individual and family as to whether the sacrament might be received regularly. Some parents and guardians are strongly opposed to their child's receiving the sacrament of reconciliation. Two factors are usually at work here. First is the concern that an individual may not be capable of understanding this sacrament. This may be true in some cases, but the child or adult may still be welcomed into the confessional for a special blessing from the priest.

However, because this sacrament offers such a beautiful opportunity for healing, we want to make sure that nothing unnecessarily hinders the individual from reception. For example, let's say an individual has difficulty verbalizing but does have a sense of right and wrong and knows when he or she has done something wrong. A written examination of conscience, prepared with the help of a parent or guardian, can be taken into the confessional to help the priest guide the conversation.

For example, if a student goes in with a sealed envelope containing a list of sins, maybe something like, "I hit my little brother even though Mom said not to," then the priest could ask, "Oh, do you sometimes hit your little brother?" The individual could then easily respond with his or her "yes" or "no" signal. If the individual has difficulty remembering in what order he or she must say things, then a simple storyboard can be taken in as a reminder, or the priest may guide the individual through the celebration of the sacrament.

However, in some cases the individual truly does not have the mental capacity to understand right or wrong and cannot understand what is happening in this sacrament. In this case, he or she should not be forced to go through the motions against his or her will, but should be welcomed to come in and pray with the priest and receive a blessing if he or she desires.

Another concern raised by parents and guardians when preparing for this sacrament is whether their child will be made to feel bad about him/herself. The problem here is one of proper catechesis and the need to prepare both the parents and the priest who will be celebrating the sacrament beforehand. In terms of proper catechesis, the opportunity for a child to receive the sacrament of reconciliation should be presented to parents or guardians in such a way that they should see it as a unique opportunity to encounter God's love and mercy—a unique opportunity available to their child. The objective here is twofold—first, to make sure the child is not excluded from reception of a sacrament he or she wishes to receive, and second, that the child is not excluded from an opportunity for grace.

To prepare the priest beforehand, it may be helpful to tell him a little bit about the individuals who will be coming to him for first reconciliation. This can include something about their disabilities and if there are any specific concerns, such as if one of the students will need a parent to accompany him or her to make the experience less anxious or if a certain student may struggle to stay sitting in one place in the confessional. It is important to ensure that the priest is on the same page as the catechist and students and that he is a priest who will be patient with the students, showing them God's love and mercy. We were blessed with two truly remarkable, compassionate priests at the parish where we ran the Children of St. Angela Merici program—and it made all the difference!

EUCHARIST

The Eucharist is the summit and pinnacle of all the other sacraments, for through it we are united to God in a way that is more intimate than any other way possible in this lifetime. The Eucharist is also the most talked about, most controversial topic when it comes to the discussion of sacramental preparation for individuals with disabilities. For many years it was thought that most individuals with mental and developmental disabilities were incapable of receiving the Eucharist, since they could not verbalize their belief in it.

This has changed in recent years and is now left to the discretion of the catechist and pastor to determine whether an individual can recognize that what is being received is more than mere bread. However, this determination is pretty open-ended. Ultimately, when in doubt, the decision should always be made in favor of the right of the baptized to receive the sacraments. (For more guidelines, see the aforementioned *Guidelines for the Celebration of the Sacraments with Persons with Disabilities.*)

When preparing an individual with mental or developmental disabilities to receive the Eucharist for the first time, plenty of time with Jesus in the tabernacle or monstrance is essential. Good, strong catechesis on the Eucharist is important and might even be done in the presence of Jesus in the Blessed Sacrament. But equally important is helping the individual with a disability develop a living relationship with Christ.

Spending time with Jesus in the Eucharist is also important because some individuals, especially those with mental disabilities, may struggle to grasp the various doctrines being taught. In these instances it is especially important to couple catechesis with experience. By allowing these individuals to experience God's grace firsthand, you allow God to work in their hearts in ways you, as a catechist, are unable to do. Time accumulated with Jesus in this way makes him a familiar presence when he is received in the Eucharist. This familiarity with Christ is something that runs even deeper than what you may be able to see on the surface. Rest assured, though, one cannot come away from time with Jesus in the Eucharist without being changed in some way.

As for doctrine, several important points should be expressed when preparing an individual with special needs to receive the Eucharist for the first time. First and foremost is the doctrine of the Real Presence. Simply put, it is essential that the individual be taught that the bread is no longer bread and the wine is no longer wine; they have become the Body and Blood of Christ and we know this because Jesus promised this, and he always keeps his promises.

As previously mentioned, precision is essential when expressing what occurs in the Eucharist. The words *bread* and *wine* shouldn't be used to reference the Body and Blood. Rather, the Eucharist should be called the Body and Blood of Jesus, or simply Jesus. In the Children of St. Angela Merici program, something we found effective was to point at the tabernacle or a picture of the Eucharist each time we saw it and ask, "Who is that? Who lives there?" All the students quickly learned to respond, "Jesus!" This is the most important doctrine to impart, and if you focus on no other teaching but this one, you will have come to the heart of the matter.

Other teachings you may want to incorporate into your

lesson planning include the origin of the Eucharist with the story of the Last Supper, as well as a connection to the love and sacrifice of Christ on the cross and a discussion of the Mass and parts of the Mass.

A number of considerations should be kept in mind when it comes to the actual reception of Jesus in the Eucharist. Some individuals have difficulty with eating and may have to receive only a particle of the Body of Christ, or only the Blood of Christ. Others may have difficulty consuming anything unfamiliar. With these individuals it may be necessary to practice with unconsecrated hosts, explaining that although this *tastes* like Communion, it is only bread, but when they receive the Eucharist, it will be Jesus. In fact, it's a good idea to engage in a similar practice with all students with special needs; they will be calmer on the day of their first Communion if they have frequently practiced the mechanics of receiving the Eucharist.

Occasionally you will have a case in which, despite all your preparation, things do not go as planned. For example, a student has a meltdown and is unable to remain in church for the rest of their first-Communion Mass. Emphasize the positive when these things happen, and do your best to calm all involved. Remember, when you have prepared a student to receive the Eucharist, your work is never in vain. Whenever he or she is ready, that individual can receive the Eucharist; and it will happen in God's time, not our own, which holds true for any of the sacraments.

CONFIRMATION

In the sacrament of confirmation, the confirmandi are sealed with the gift of the Holy Spirit. This sacrament completes what is begun at baptism and is essential and instrumental to the living out of life in the Church. Because of this, the sacrament of confirmation should be offered to all, regardless of disability. (See the *Catechism of the Catholic Church*, 1302–1307, for more on this sacrament.)

Ideally, individuals with disabilities should be afforded the opportunity to undergo formal preparation for this sacrament. This preparation should include prayer to the Holy Spirit. In the Children of St. Angela Merici program, all students preparing for confirmation were taught to pray "Come, Holy Spirit" over and over again. It is important that those preparing for the sacrament are taught to pray that they long for the coming of the Holy Spirit. Even such a simple prayer as this helps prepare these individuals.

A number of different components can and should be included in a preparation program for confirmation. First, tell the story of Pentecost. A connection should be made between that first coming of the Holy Spirit to the Church and the coming of the Holy Spirit upon an individual when the sacrament of confirmation is received. A confirmation curriculum should also include a unit on the sacrament of baptism, the sacrament in which those preparing for confirmation first received the Holy Spirit. There is a link between these two sacraments of initiation!

A unit on the gifts of the Holy Spirit (with particular emphasis on the gifts and the joy of receiving a gift) helps the students anticipate what they will be receiving. Finally, a unit on the sacrament itself—matter, form, and rite—helps the students know what to expect and what will be expected of them. All of these lessons and units can be accompanied by pictures and other visual aids, such as figurines or pictures of the Apostles when telling the story of Pentecost and visits to the church to see the chrism oil and baptismal font. Most important, the emphasis should be on the joyful expectation of the coming of the Holy Spirit. If those preparing to receive the sacrament have grasped that lesson, they are well prepared.

Rite of Christian Initiation of Adults and Special Situations

Unique situations often arise when preparing individuals with disabilities to receive the sacraments. First, we have the adult individual with mental or developmental disabilities who expresses a desire to enter the Church. Most parish RCIA programs are not set up to meet this individual's unique needs. However, I strongly encourage all such programs to welcome a person with disabilities into their midst. With the help of the pastor and the director of religious education, some modifications can be made to help this individual prepare to receive the sacraments. In time, I hope more programs specifically tailored to meet the needs of individuals with disabilities looking to join the Church will be made available.

Some situations may arise that are unique to the culture of adult individuals with mental or developmental disabilities. Many of these individuals are old enough that they no longer have parents or relatives who can attest to their sacramental record. Furthermore, many of these individuals may have lived in an institution at a younger age or may never have belonged to a parish, and so it can be impossible to trace their sacramental records.

These same individuals may now find themselves in a Catholic parish or small faith-sharing community and desire to be included in the sacramental life of the community. Every effort should be made to trace their sacramental history, and if it cannot be located, be open to doing a conditional baptism (administered with much celebration and joy in the midst of the community). The reception of other sacraments could then follow.

Some would prescribe to letting all people with disabilities, regardless of creed, receive the Eucharist when they attend Mass. The thought behind this is that, because these individuals face rejection in so many other areas of life, we should do what we can to prevent their being excluded from what is happening at Mass.

I believe we do a disservice to individuals with disabilities when we have them receive Communion just so they feel included. The Eucharist is about so much more than that, and we should want them to share in the fullness of what the Eucharist is. This means that if an individual is not Catholic, or his or her guardians do not wish the person to become Catholic, it is more respectful to who they are and what their family's faith may be not to have them receive Communion. This is not about excluding them, but rather about including them in a way that is true to their own personal beliefs, as well as to what the Eucharist itself means. For example, let's say we have a Baptist woman with mental disabilities who has joined our Catholic faith-sharing group for people with disabilities because she enjoys the community and fellowship. How beautiful! We would be right to welcome her.

However, it's important to honor her beliefs and include her in such a way that is in keeping with those beliefs, even if she is still learning what those beliefs are. A Baptist does not profess faith in the Real Presence, and though we can share our beliefs, we cannot force her to believe what we believe. If she chooses to attend a Mass with her Catholic faith-sharing group, we should encourage her to enjoy listening to the Scriptures, which is a significant way she encounters Christ in her particular denomination. If we don't want to exclude her during Communion, we should welcome her to come forward and receive a heartfelt blessing from the priest. This would let her know she is welcome and beloved of Jesus without going against what either of us believe about the Eucharist. While it is true that the Eucharist is a sacrament in which we fully encounter Christ, it's also the sacrament that expresses our full unity with the Church. If we ignore the latter half of this, we're missing something significant from the meaning of the sacrament.

Let's say, however, that this Baptist woman really comes to believe in what we are talking about in our Catholic faith-sharing group and desires to receive the Eucharist because she wants Jesus. Clearly, God is calling her to share in the life of the sacraments. If her parents or guardians give their consent, we should formally welcome her into the Catholic Church and prepare her for first Communion. However, if they will not give their consent, it is our responsibility to do all we can to advocate for this woman and help her parents to see how real her desire is to join the Church. We must allow this to happen in God's time, not ours.

Our real concern here is wanting what is real and genuine for individuals with mental and developmental disabilities. To give them Communion without welcoming them into the Church just so they "feel included" is usually well intentioned, but it is missing something. It does not solve the problem of inclusion, it only makes them *feel* like the problem is solved. If we truly want them to feel welcome and included, then we must do it in a way that is in keeping with where God has led them thus far. That means if they are not Catholic, we include them in a way that is respectful of their faith tradition, and if they desire to become Catholic, we do all we can to help them realize their desire.

Ultimately, when considering these various unique situations, it is best to handle them with much care and prayer, and to do so in consultation with your parish's pastor and diocese.

Sharing in the Fullness—A Vision

In the work of sacramental preparation, we must bear in mind our overall vision—to help those with disabilities share in the fullness of the faith. This is about more than inclusion, more than helping those with disabilities through the same rites of passage as their counterparts without disabilities; it's about helping them on their way to heaven. We welcome them to receive the sacraments because these are the beautiful gifts Jesus left his Church to help us on the way to heaven. Through the sacraments we grow in holiness and grow closer to that perfect union we hope one day to have with Christ. Through the grace of these sacraments, those with disabilities can live out their unique vocations and one day, God willing, become the saints God is calling them to be.

Epilogue

As I finish writing this book, the Church is in the beautiful season of Advent—a time of joyful hope and deep longing for Christ. I cannot think of a more fitting backdrop for reflecting on the significance of doing ministry for those with disabilities.

In the Incarnation, God became man to redeem us and save us from our sins. However, what is particularly remarkable is how this was done. God chose to be born of a humble, poor virgin in a stable. He chose to come to us as an infant, the smallest and weakest or most vulnerable among us. He chose to announce his birth first to shepherds, not kings. There is something significant in the way this came to be—God truly came for the little and the lowly.

What a powerful message this is for all those who are little and lowly in the eyes of the world. What a message of hope this is for all who have known rejection, who have been looked down upon or been belittled. This revelation brings great joy to those who may feel unimportant. In God's eyes, those who are the littlest and most forgotten are the most precious. It is these whom God calls to accomplish his will in a special way.

Those with disabilities and special needs in the Church are truly God's beloved, called by Christ to carry out God's beautiful will for their lives. To do this, they need the support of the Church, the welcome of her members, and the grace and strength that come from the sacraments. Those with special needs and disabilities need the Church's help, but more important, we need their help. We need them to remind us that God chooses those the world looks down on. We need them to remind us that God works through those the world finds to be little and weak in incredible ways.

As you read these words, somewhere in the world a little baby lies sleeping—a little baby born into this world with a disability of some sort. What will this child's place be in the Church? Those reading these words are called to ensure that this child has a home in the Church. For just as God called a poor and humble virgin more than two thousand years ago, God still chooses those who are little and weak, the forgotten and the unexpected, to be saints.

Additional Resources

Congregation for the Clergy. General Directory for Catechesis. Washington: United States Catholic Conference, 1998.

Foley, Edward, et al. *Developmental Disabilities and Sacramental Access—New Paradigms for Sacramental Encounters.* Collegeville: The Liturgical Press, 1994.

Harding, Grace T., et al. *The Rose Fitzgerald Kennedy Program to Improve Catholic Religious Education for Children and Adults with Mental Retardation—A Comprehensive Developmental Curriculum.* Pittsburgh: Slavia Printing, 1996.

Harrington, Sr. Mary Therese. *A Place for All: Mental Retardation, Catechesis and Liturgy.* Collegeville: The Liturgical Press, 1992.

Harrington, Sr. Mary Therese. "Sacraments of Initiation for People with Developmental Disabilities—Pastoral Orientations and Options" handout.

National Conference of Catholic Bishops. *Guidelines for Celebration of the Sacraments with People with Disabilities.* Originally published November 1978. Online. National Catholic Partnership on Disability. http://www.ncpd.org/Sacramental%20Guidelines.htm.

"Serving Children with Disabilities." ECHOES. Volume 2, Number 2. Mount Rainier: Center for Children and Theology, 1998.

"Special Religious Education Department." Diocese of Oakland. Online. http://www.oakdiocese.org/education/spred/special-religious-education-department-2013-spred-ministry. First accessed February 27, 2009.

"SPRED—Communities of Faith Welcoming Children and Adults with Developmental Disabilities." Informational booklet. Chicago: Archdiocese of Chicago.

"SPRED's Mission Statement." SPRED—Special Religious Development—Archdiocese of Chicago. (Handout)

"SPRED—Special Religious Development." Archdiocese of Chicago. Online. http://www.spred.org/. Accessed February 15, 2009.

USCCB. *National Directory for Catechesis.* Washington: United States Conference of Catholic Bishops, 1991.

"Welcoming Parishioners with Disabilities." http://www.usccbpublishing.org/searchproducts.cfm. USCCB Publishing website. Accessed March 10, 2009.

Parish Resource Handbooks from Liguori Publications

Handbook for Today's Catechist is the best-selling resource that explores many aspects of the role of catechist in a classroom setting, at home, and in the parish community. In an easy-to-understand format, this handbook provides an overview of the Bible, the life and teaching of Jesus, the mission of the Church in continuing Jesus' ministry, liturgy, and sacrament, and how to be a moral example to those we teach. An up-to-date guide for the catechist, this book looks at the challenge of catechizing children in the age of computers and electronics and how to identify good or misleading information on the Internet. It includes a lesson-plan outline, as well as some basic "dos & don'ts" associated with teaching the faith.

English: 9780764-818462
Adapted for Spanish: 9780764-818714

As a supplement, Liguori offers the *Handbook of Sacraments for Today's Catechist,* covering material that is useful for instruction on all sacraments at different age levels and includes sections just for the catechists who are preparing children for Penance, Eucharist, or Confirmation. There are a variety of stories that provide a way for the catechist to introduce topics, giving children something to relate to in order to learn theological concepts, and ways to reach out to families to continue the learning process at home.

English: 9780764-819469

In today's Church, an increasing number of laypeople participate in parish ministry. *Handbook for Today's Parish Leaders* gives leaders the spiritual guidance they look for and the practical advice they need to be a leader. It provides a firm foundation and lots of practical tips for responding to the call to serve, developing leadership and collaboration skills, and empowering others to lead.

English: 9780764-820014
Adapted for Spanish: 9780764-820489

**To order, visit your local bookstore
or call 800-325-9521 or visit us at liguori.org**